D1090927

Rookie
National Parks™

Olympic
National Park

by Audra Wallace

Content Consultant
National Park Service

Reading Consultant
Jeanne M. Clidas, Ph.D.
Reading Specialist

Children's Press®
An Imprint of Scholastic Inc.

Library of Congress Cataloging-in-Publication Data
Names: Wallace, Audra, author.
Title: Olympic National Park/by Audra Wallace.
Description: New York, NY: Children's Press, an imprint of Scholastic Inc.,
2018. | Series: Rookie national parks | Includes index.
Identifiers: LCCN 2017023148 | ISBN 9780531231968 (library binding) |
ISBN 9780531230954 (pbk.)
Subjects: LCSH: Olympic National Park (Wash.)—Juvenile literature.
Classification: LCC F897.O5 W35 2018 | DDC 979.7/98—dc23
LC record available at https://lccn.loc.gov/2017023148

Produced by Spooky Cheetah Press
Design: Judith Christ-Lafond/Ed LoPresti Graphic Design

Published in 2018 by Children's Press, an imprint of Scholastic Inc.

Printed in Heshan, China 62

SCHOLASTIC, CHILDREN'S PRESS™, ROOKIE NATIONAL PARKS™, and
associated logos are trademarks and/or registered trademarks of Scholastic Inc.

1 2 3 4 5 6 7 8 9 10 R 27 26 25 24 23 22 21 20 19 18

Scholastic, Inc., 557 Broadway, New York, NY 10012

Photos ©: cover: dkroner/Shutterstock; back cover: Danita Delimont Stock/AWL Images;
cartoon fox throughout: Bill Mayer; 1-2: PCRex/Shutterstock; 3: OGphoto/iStockphoto;
4-5: Spring Images/Alamy Images; 6-7 background: Kirkendall-Spring Photographers/Minden
Pictures; 7 inset: Aurora Photos/Alamy Images; 8-9: Stas Moroz/Shutterstock; 10 inset: Diez,
O./picture alliance/Arco Images G/Newscom; 10-11: Alvis Upitis/Media Bakery; 12-13: Colin
D. Young/Shutterstock; 13 inset: Ingemar Magnusson/Dreamstime; 14: Michael Hanson/Getty
Images; 15 background: Steve Whiston/Fallen Log Photograhy/Getty Images; 15 inset: Andrew
Geiger/Getty Images; 16 background-17: robertharding/Alamy Images; 16 inset: Jordan
Siemens/Getty Images; 18: Greg Probst/DanitaDelimont.com/Newscom; 19: Rob Tilley/NPL/
Minden Pictures; 20-21 background: Steven J. Kazlowski/Alamy Images; 21 inset: FLPA/ Bob
Gibbons/age fotostock; 22-23 background: Gerry Ellis/age fotostock; 23 top: Suzi Eszterhas/
age fotostock; 23 bottom: Dominique Braud/Dembinsky Photo Associates/Alamy Images;
24 background-25: IakovKalinin/iStockphoto; 24 top: Aaron Mccoy/Media Bakery; 24 bottom:
Aurora Photos/Alamy Images; 26 top left: Musat/iStockphoto; 26 top center: andyKRAKOVSKI/
iStockphoto; 26 top right: GlobalP/iStockphoto; 26 bottom left: GlobalP/iStockphoto; 26 bottom
center: Michael Sewell/Getty Images; 26 bottom right: Justin Bailie/Media Bakery; 27 top left:
Copyright Michael Cummings/Getty Images; 27 top center: Joel Sartore/National Geographic
Photo Ark/Getty Images; 27 top right: naturediver/iStockphoto; 27 bottom left: narvikk/
iStockphoto; 27 bottom center: Dorling Kindersley/Getty Images; 27 bottom right: Joel Sartore/
National Geographic Photo Ark/Getty Images; 30 top left: heibaihui/Getty Images; 30 top
right: Matthew Maran/NPL/Minden Pictures; 30 bottom left: Nature Photographers Ltd/Alamy
Images; 30 bottom right: Martin B Withers/FLPA/Minden Pictures; 31 top: elmvilla/iStockphoto;
31 center top: Velvetfish/iStockphoto; 31 center bottom: Juliengrondin/Dreamstime; 31 bottom:
Bütow/ullstein bild/Getty Images; 32: Floris van Breugel/NPL/Minden Pictures.

Maps by Jim McMahon.

Table of Contents

I am Ranger Red Fox, your tour guide. Are you ready for an amazing adventure in Olympic?

Welcome to Olympic National Park!

Olympic is in Washington State. It was made a **national park** in 1938. People visit national parks to explore nature.

The Pacific Ocean surrounds the park on three sides. There is plenty to see and do here.

United States

←Washington

Olympic
National Park

Olympic National Park has many different areas to explore. You can hike around snowcapped mountains. You can follow a trail through a rain forest. You can even look for sea stars in tide pools.

It is about 5 miles (8 km) to the top of Mount Olympus.

More than 12,000 years ago, Native Americans hunted in this area.

Up to 167 inches (424 centimeters) of rain falls in Olympic's rain forests each year!

Hoh Rain Forest

Chapter 1

Wet and Wild

You may be surprised to learn there are rain forests in Olympic. A rain forest is one that gets more than 80 inches (203 centimeters) of rain each year.

Tropical rain forests are found near the equator, where it is hot. Temperate rain forests are found in cooler regions—like Olympic.

Some of the trees in Olympic's rain forests are more than 200 feet (61 meters) tall. They include western hemlock and Douglas fir. The world's biggest Sitka (**sit**-ka) spruce also grows here. Maple and red alder trees are found in the park, too. Their leaves brighten the forest with different colors in the fall.

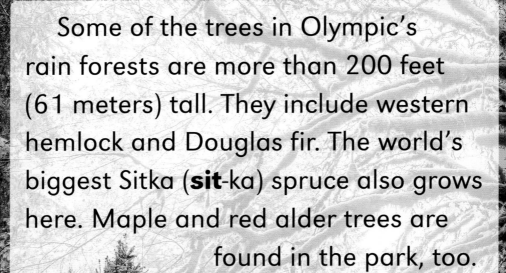

The western hemlock is Washington's state tree.

Thick layers of moss cling to the trees. Ferns cover the damp rain forest floor.

Many of the trees in Olympic's rain forests are hundreds of years old.

Some of the park's beaches are sandy. Others are rocky.

12

Chapter 2

Down by the Seashore

Olympic National Park has more than 70 miles (113 kilometers) of coastline.

Ruby Beach is the most popular beach in the park. It is named for the ruby-like crystals that are mixed in with the sand.

Rubies are special stones often used in jewelry.

In some spots, tall towers of rock stick up from the sand. Some of these sea stacks can be more than

If visitors want to take a dip, they can head to Lake Crescent.

40 feet (12 meters) tall. The wind and waves wear away the sides of the rocks. They make the sea stacks into different shapes.

People do not swim in the ocean. The water is too cold. They look for sea stars and crabs in tide pools.

Some sea stacks are about as tall as four school buses stacked on top of each other.

If a sea star loses an arm, it can grow a new one.

Snowshoeing is a great way to see the park in winter.

Blue Glacier is big enough to cover about 40 football fields.

Chapter 3

Mighty Mountains

Giant mountains rise into the clouds over the park. Some are covered by **glaciers**. The most famous is Blue Glacier.

Blue Glacier covers part of Mount Olympus, the tallest peak in the park. Mount Olympus is 7,980 feet (2,432 meters) tall. Only well-trained climbers are allowed to climb it.

Rivers and streams rush down Olympic's mountains. Some water gushes over rocky cliffs as waterfalls. One is called Sol Duc Falls. It flows into hot springs.

Hot springs are special pools of water. They are heated by **magma**

These are the hot springs at Sol Duc.

underground. The hot springs are like big warm baths. People soak in them to relax.

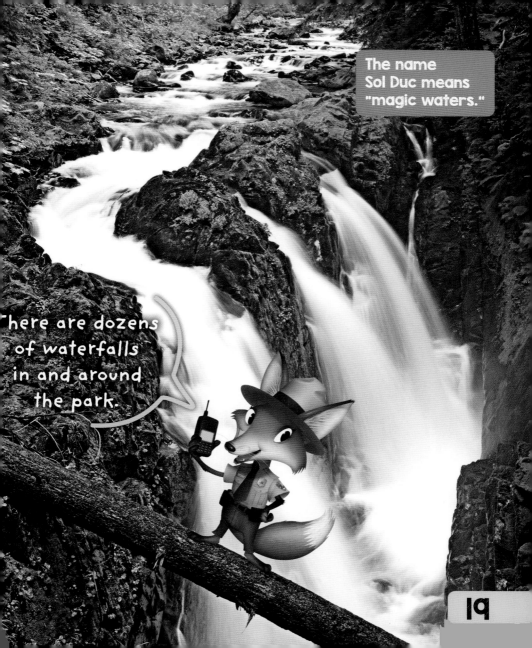

The name Sol Duc means "magic waters."

There are dozens of waterfalls in and around the park.

Chapter 4

Wonderful Wildlife

Olympic National Park is packed with wildlife. Black bears wander near the park's rivers. Roosevelt elk graze on ferns. Spotted owls peek out from the trees. Slimy banana slugs glide across the ground.

Banana slugs can grow to about 10 inches (25 cm) long.

Down by the sea, bald eagles soar overhead. They nest in trees along the beaches. Sea otters float on thick **kelp**.

In the ocean, Pacific harbor seals rest on small islands. In the distance, orcas swim among the waves.

Pacific harbor seals can stay underwater for up to 30 minutes.

Sea otters wrap themselves in kelp so that they don't float away.

The park has hundreds of awesome bridges.

Visitors to Olympic like to fish for trout.

Olympic National Park is often called "the gift from the sea." More than three million people visit it each year. From the rain forests to the coast, there is so much to explore!

Imagine you could visit Olympic. What would you do there?

These are just some of the incredible animals that make their home in Olympic.

beaver

coho salmon

mink

mountain lion

spotted owl

Roosevelt elk

Wildlife by the Numbers

The park is home to about...

300 types of birds   **56** types of mammals

The Olympic torrent salamander is one of three animals found only in this park!

snowshoe hare

sea otter

Pacific tree frog

bald eagle

black bear

Olympic torrent salamander

20 types of reptiles and amphibians

37 native fish species

Where Is Ranger Red Fox?

Oh no! Ranger Red Fox has lost his way in the park. But you can help. Use the map and the clues below to find him.

1. Ranger Red Fox fell asleep on Ruby Beach.

2. Then he headed northeast along a river. He ended up in a rain forest.

3. Next, he headed north. He paddled around a lake shaped like a crescent.

4. Finally, he hiked south to the tallest mountain in the park.

Help! Can you find me?

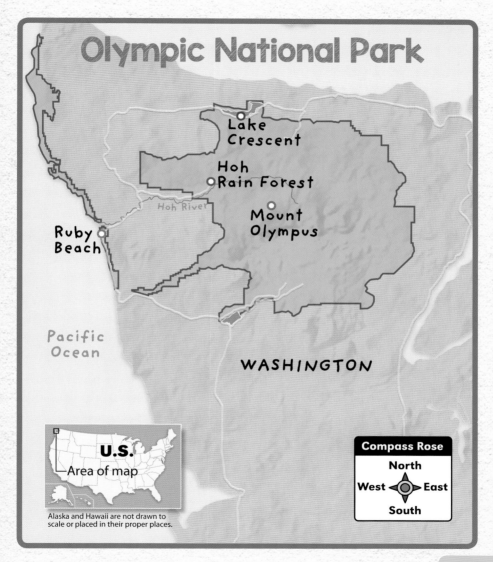

Olympic National Park

Lake Crescent

Hoh Rain Forest

Hoh River

Mount Olympus

Ruby Beach

Pacific Ocean

WASHINGTON

U.S.
Area of map

Alaska and Hawaii are not drawn to scale or placed in their proper places.

Compass Rose

North
West ◆ East
South

Answer: Mount Olympus

Leaf Tracker

Can you guess which leaf belongs to which tree in Olympic? Read the clues to help you.

A.

I. Western hemlock
Clue: This tree's needlelike leaves are short and flat.

B.

2. Big-leaf maple
Clue: This tree's leaves are shiny and wide. They have five "fingers."

3. Sitka spruce
Clue: This tree's needlelike leaves are stiff and sharp.

C.

4. Red alder
Clue: The leaves of this tree are oval-shaped with pointy tips.

D.

30

Answers: 1. C; 2. A; 3. B; 4. D

Glossary

glaciers (**glay**-shurz):
huge blocks of
slow-moving ice

kelp (kelp):
large, edible brown
seaweed

magma (**mag**-muh):
melted rock found beneath
Earth's surface; becomes lava
when it flows out of volcanoes

national park (**nash**-uh-nuhl
pahrk): area where the land
and its animals are protected
by the U.S. government

Index

Facts for Now

Visit this Scholastic Web site for more information on Olympic National Park:
www.factsfornow.scholastic.com
Enter the keyword Olympic

About the Author

Audra Wallace is an editor at Scholastic. She lives with her family in New York. She enjoys going on adventures to different places with them.